Huge machines are used at construction sites

A Construction Site

Melissa Gish

A⁺

Smart Apple Media

COPYRIGHT

Published by Smart Apple Media

1980 Lookout Drive, North Mankato, MN 56003

Designed by Rita Marshall

Copyright © 2004 Smart Apple Media. International copyright reserved in all countries. No part of this book may be reproduced in any form without written permission from the publisher.

Printed in the United States of America

Photographs by Corbis (Dale C. Spartas), Image Finders (Jim Baron, Eric R. Berndt), Tom Myers, Tom Stack & Associates (Thomas Kitchin, Novastock, Tom & Therisa Stack, Greg Vaughn)

Library of Congress Cataloging-in-Publication Data

Gish, Melissa. A construction site / by Melissa Gish.

p. cm. – (Field trips) Includes bibliographical references and index.

Summary: Briefly describes what goes on at different construction sites, people who work on construction crews, and some of the heavy machines used. Includes a related activity.

ISBN 1-58340-323-X

1. Building sites—Juvenile literature. 2. Building—Juvenile literature. [1. Building. 2. Construction equipment.] I. Title. II. Field trips (Smart Apple Media) (Mankato, Minn.).

TH375.G57 2003   624–dc21   2002042785

First Edition 9 8 7 6 5 4 3 2 1

A Construction Site

At the Construction Site   6

The Construction Crew   12

Heavy Machines   14

New Construction   18

Hands On: Crawlers versus Wheels   22

Additional Information   24

CONTENTS

At the Construction Site

The world seems to be getting bigger every day. As cities expand, the need for construction grows. Highways and streets must be laid. Houses, apartment buildings, and bridges must be built. Construction sites are everywhere. ✑ A plan for a new street or a building is first **drafted** on paper. Then the plan is used to make a small **model**. When the people who are working on the project agree that the plan is good, construction can begin. This is not an easy job. It takes a lot of

Tall cranes are needed to build skyscrapers

people working together and a lot of special equipment to construct a new part of a town or city. The workers on a construction **crew** must be very good at their jobs. They each have an important job to do. Most construction machines are left outside without protection from rain and wind— they're so sturdy they don't need it. Because construction work is sometimes dangerous, the workers must be able to trust each other. They need to work together to keep each other safe at the construction site.

Workers stand on platforms called scaffolding

The walls of a building are often built last

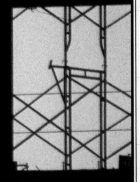

The Construction Crew

Work at a construction site starts and ends with the **foreman**. The foreman's job is to run things at the site. He or she checks to make sure that all of the workers at the site are ready to begin work. He or she plans the jobs that will be done during the day and gives each worker a task. The foreman keeps everyone organized and busy.

At 12 feet (3.7 m), the tire of the world's biggest wheel loader is more than twice as tall as a person.

Some of the workers drive big machines. They are called machine operators. In order to operate the machines safely,

workers must have the right knowledge and skills. Being a

machine operator requires special training and a license.

Because machine operators are high up off the ground,

Workers wear hard hats to protect their heads

they can't always see what to do with their machines. Other workers must guide the machine operators from the ground using radios. These workers are part of the ground crew. They tell the machine operators how deep to dig or how far to push with their machines.

M**Heavy Machines**

any different kinds of machines are used at a construction site. Two machines that work together are the wheel loader and the dump truck. A wheel loader has a deep shovel on the front, called a bucket. The wheel loader uses its

bucket to scoop up soil, rock, or other material. Then it tilts the

bucket to drop the material into the back of a dump truck. A

dump truck can hold a lot of material. When it is full, the back

A hydraulic excavator fills a dump truck

of the dump truck tilts up to dump the material out.

A bulldozer has a wide, flat shovel on its front. It uses this

front-end blade to push soil and rock. It is also used to make

the ground smooth and flat. **The first bulldozers were made by the Holt Manufacturing Company in 1904. This American company later became Caterpillar Inc.**

Bulldozers have **crawlers** instead of wheels. Unlike wheels, crawlers do not sink into soft surfaces such

as dirt or sand, and they can go up steep slopes.

The hydraulic excavator has crawlers too. It has a long limb

Bulldozers move easily over muddy ground

on the front, called the boom and arm. It works like a human arm that bends at the elbow and wrist. Different parts can be attached to the arm to do different jobs. One part is a bucket used for scooping. Another is a drill for digging holes. There's also a crusher (giant scissors) and a ripper (a giant claw).

New Construction

Construction of new roads and buildings takes place every day. Old buildings may be torn down or land may be cleared of trees to make way for new highways and buildings. Some construction projects take place in the middle of busy

cities, causing cars and trucks to move slowly around

construction areas. These projects must be done quickly,

because they can cause traffic and other problems. ⌘

Road construction must be done quickly

A construction crew moves onto a site and gets to work right away. Construction crews often work from sunrise to sunset, and may even work on Saturdays. A small construction project, such as the building of a house, may be finished in a matter of weeks. Big projects, such as the building of bridges or skyscrapers, may take years. Once the job is completed, a busy construction crew moves right on to the next project and the next construction site.

The giant magnet that can be attached to the arm of a hydraulic excavator is capable of picking up a car.

The wooden frame of a house is built first

Crawlers versus Wheels

Construction equipment must be able to move across a soft surface without sinking. Try this simple experiment to see why crawlers work better than wheels.

What You Need

A sink or dishpan

Dish soap

A penny

A dollar bill

What You Do

1. Pour some dish soap into the sink or dishpan.
2. Fill the sink or dish pan with water, stirring it with your hand so the soap makes lots of fluffy bubbles.
3. Hold the penny in one hand and the dollar bill in the other above the soapy water.
4. Drop the penny and the dollar bill.

What You See

Like the wheel of a truck, the penny drops through the soft surface of the soap bubbles. But like the belt of a crawler, the dollar bill doesn't sink. This is because the weight of the dollar bill is spread out over a larger area.

Crawlers support this hydraulic excavator

INFORMATION

Index

bulldozers 16

crawlers 16, 22

crew 8, 14, 20

dump trucks 14–15

foreman 12

hydraulic excavators 16, 20

machine operators 12–14

plans 6

wheel loaders 12, 14–15

Words to Know

crawlers (CRAW-lurz)—sheets of iron and rubber shaped like a big belt

crew (CROO)—a group of people working together

drafted (DRAF-ted)—planned out step by step in writing and drawings

foreman (FOR-man)—the leader of a group of people working together

license (LY-sens)—special permission to do something

model (MOD-ul)—a copy of something built at a much smaller size

Read More

Bial, Raymond. *The Houses*. Salt Lake City, Utah: Benchmark Books, 2001.

Imershein, Betsy. *Construction Trucks*. New York: Little Simon, 2000.

Schaefer, Lola M. *Construction Sites*. Crystal Lake, Ill.: Heinemann Library, 2000.

Stone, Lynn M. *Roads and Highways*. Vero Beach, Fla.: Rourke Book Company, 2002.

Internet Sites

B4UBuild Stuff 4 Kids
http://www.b4ubuild.com/kids/index.html

Bob the Builder
http://www.bobthebuilder.org

Construction Buddies
http://www.constructionbuddies.com

The Historical Construction Equipment Association of Canada
http://www.bigtoy.com